GUO PEI
COUTURE FANTASY

A Coloring Book

T0340634

GUO PEI
COUTURE FANTASY

A Coloring Book

Fine Arts Museums of San Francisco
Distributed by Yale University Press,
New Haven and London

Guo Pei sketching a design for her collection Alternate Universe (Fall/Winter 2019–2020), Beijing, 2018

GUO PEI
SKETCHING FASHION

Guo Pei, China's premier couturier and one of the world's most innovative fashion designers, has captivated the fashion world for more than twenty-five years. Her extraordinary designs, featuring a rich layering of sculptural silhouettes and surface embellishments, are renowned for their exquisite craftsmanship and lavish embroidery.

Guo Pei studied fashion illustration in the 1980s, while a student at Beijing Second Light Industry School, where drawing was a focus of the fashion design program. Her sketches reveal her to be a skilled and confident draftsperson, capable of rendering the finest details as well as conveying concepts with broad, impressionistic lines that capture the essence of her ideas.

The designer established her own design house, Rose Studio, in 1997. She begins a new collection by illustrating each design, using her drawing skills to impart her creative ideas to her team of artisans and patternmakers. Simple outlines are enlivened by gradually adding detail, ornamentation, and sometimes color. Each sketch is an artwork in its own right, providing an invaluable glimpse into a design's beginnings as a line drawing on paper before its eventual materialization as a sumptuous dress.

The sketches in this coloring book invite aspiring fashion designers to collaborate directly with Guo Pei's design process. Many of the sketches are previously unpublished, and all are drawn from some of the designer's most cherished collections.

Draw and color your own fashion sketch here!

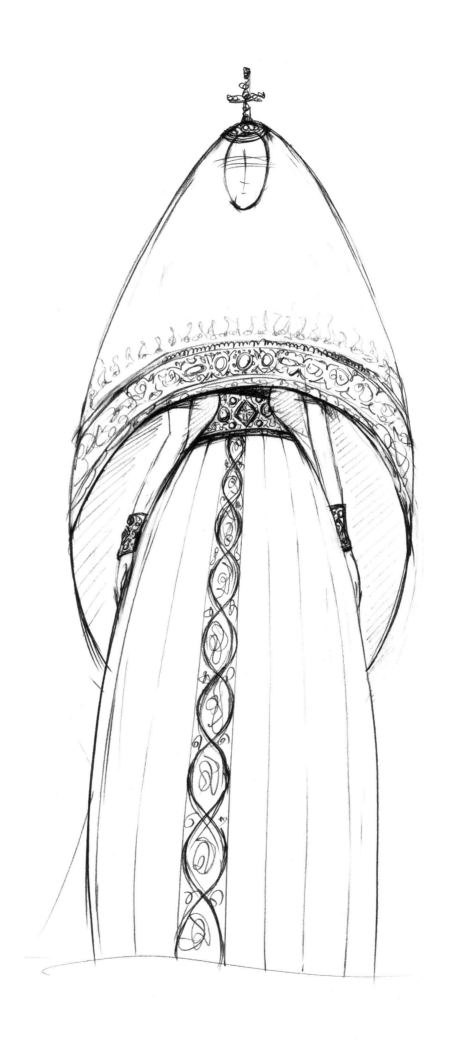

Draw and color your own fashion sketch here!

Draw and color your own fashion sketch here!

Draw and color your own fashion sketch here!

Draw and color your own fashion sketch here!

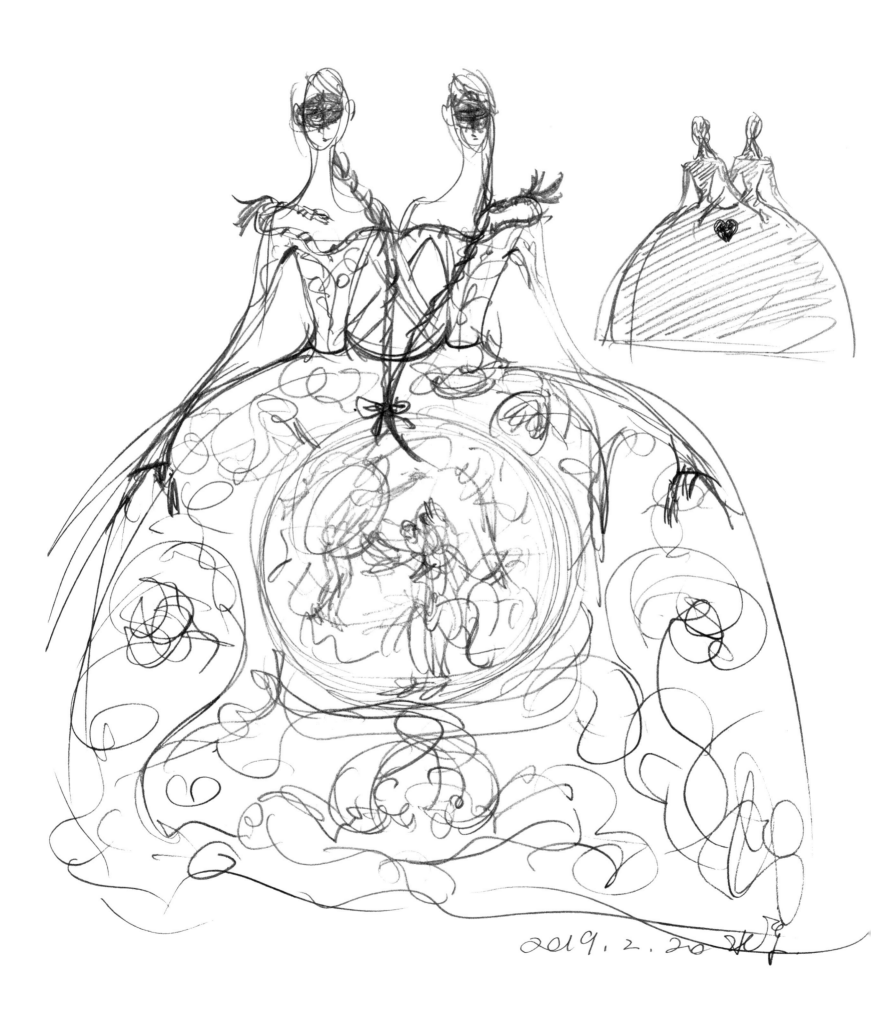

2019. 2. 20

Draw and color your own fashion sketch here!

Draw and color your own fashion sketch here!

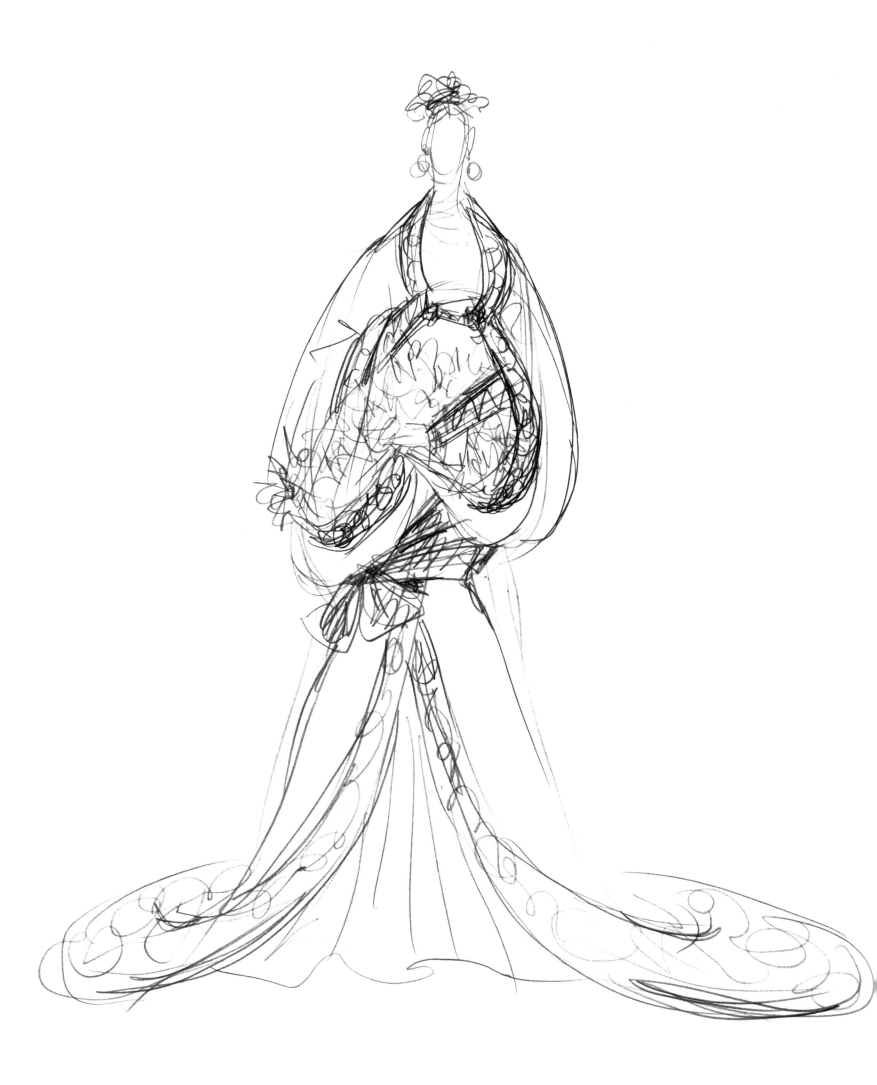

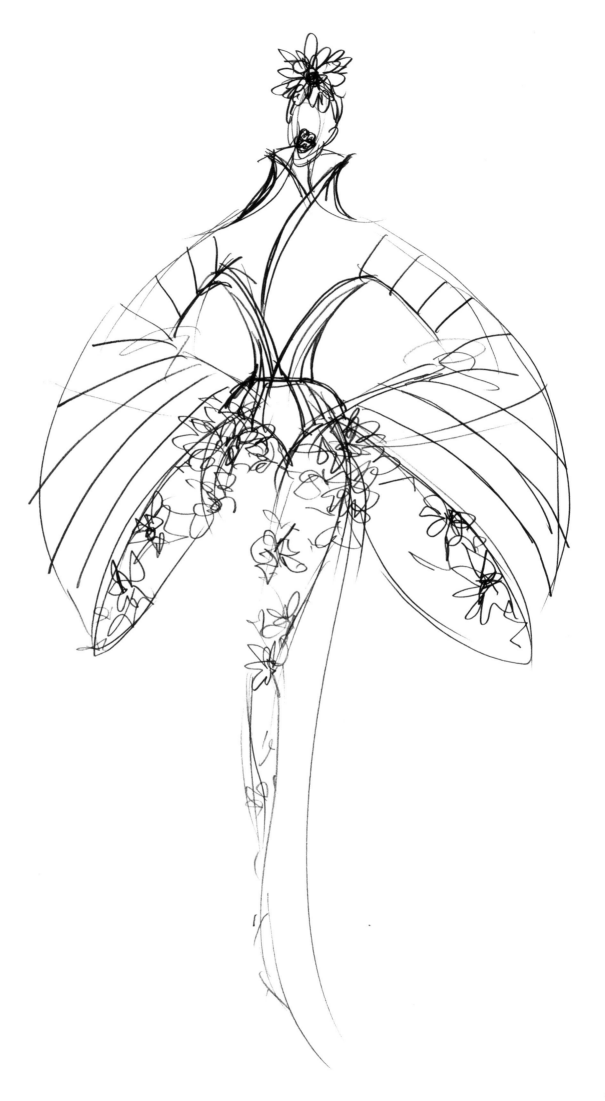

Published by the Fine Arts Museums of San Francisco and
distributed by Yale University Press on the occasion of the exhibition

COUTURE FANTASY

at the Legion of Honor, San Francisco,
from April 16 to September 5, 2022

This coloring book is produced in collaboration with Guo Pei
and facilitated by the Asian Couture Federation.

Guo Pei   ACF | Asian Couture Federation

Copyright © 2022 Fine Arts Museums of San Francisco.
Artwork copyright © Guo Pei / Asian Couture Federation

All rights reserved. No part of this publication may be reproduced,
stored in a retrieval system, or transmitted in any form or by
any means, electronic, mechanical, photocopying, recording,
or otherwise without prior written consent of the publishers.

ISBN: 978-0-300-26579-8

Yale University Press
P.O. Box 209040
302 Temple Street
New Haven, CT 06520-9040
yalebooks.com/art

Fine Arts Museums of San Francisco
de Young, Golden Gate Park
50 Hagiwara Tea Garden Drive
San Francisco, CA 94118-4502
famsf.org

Jill D'Alessandro, curator in charge of costume and textile arts
Stuart Hata, director of retail operations
Leslie Dutcher, director of publications

Edited by Lesley Bruynesteyn
Picture research by José Jovel
Designed and typeset by Yvonne Tsang
Color separations, printing, and binding by Verona Libri, Italy

The text on p. 5 is adapted from *Guo Pei: Couture Fantasy*,
edited by Jill D'Alessandro, and published by the Fine Arts Museums
of San Francisco in association with Yale University Press in 2022.

PICTURE CREDITS

Cover, 2, 7–10, back cover: Garden of Soul, 2015. 1, 14–16, 18, 48: An Amazing Journey in a Childhood Dream, 2007. 4: courtesy of Guo Pei. 12–13: Samsara, 2006. 17, 19–23, 47: Legends, Spring/Summer 2017. 24, 26–27: Elysium, Spring/Summer 2018. 29–31: L'Architecture, Fall/Winter 2018–2019. 32, 35: East Palace, Spring/Summer 2019. 36–37, 39–40: Alternate Universe, Fall/Winter 2019–2020. 42–46: Himalaya, Spring/Summer 2020.